— KINDFULLY ME SERIES —

KIND WISHES

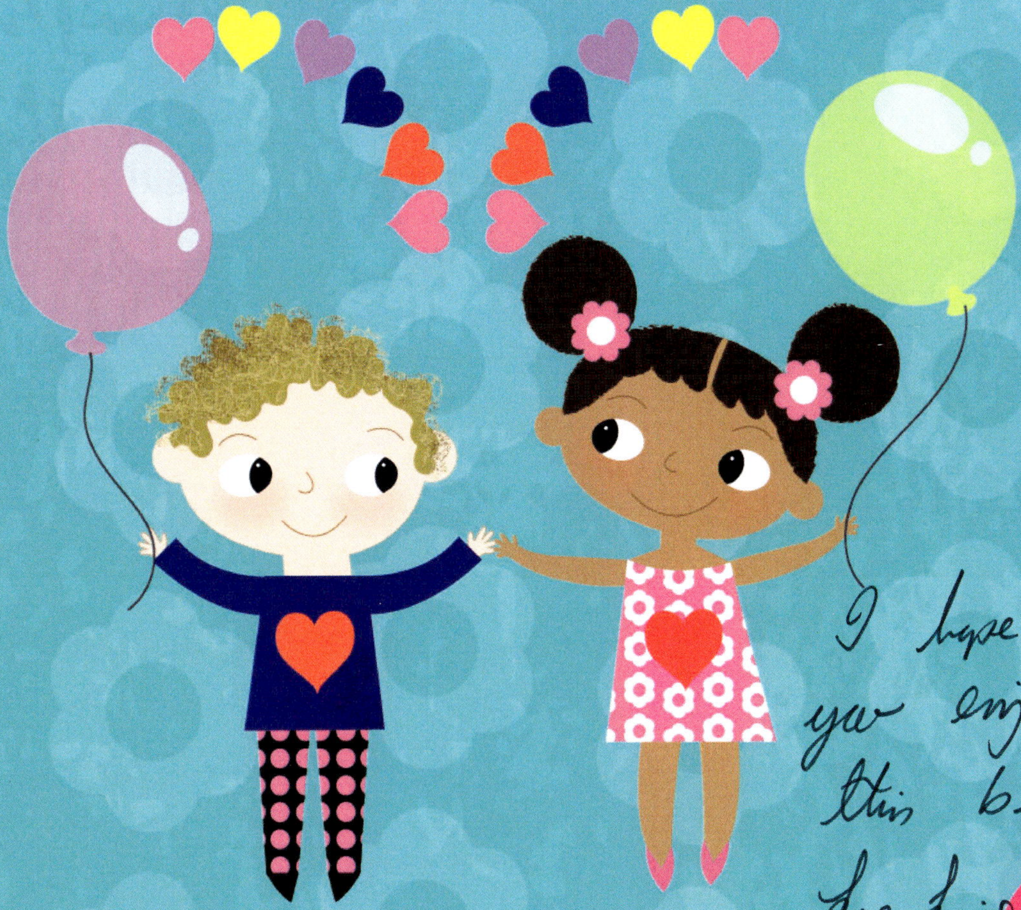

I hope that you enjoy this book Love Louise

Book 1

Louise Shanagher
Úna Woods

About the Author

Louise Shanagher is a children's therapist, mindfulness teacher and trainer. Louise has a BA and MSc in Psychology and further qualifications in Play Therapy and Mindfulness. She is the creator of the 'Creative Mindfulness Kids' method and has trained hundreds of people to be children's mindfulness teachers.

She is the author of six books: The 'Mindfully Me' series, Ireland's first series of mindfulness books for children and the 'Kindfully Me' series. Louise is passionate about promoting positive mental health for children and young people. She believes that all children should get the opportunity to learn how to practise mindfulness and self compassion and believes that these practices will help children lead happier, healthier and more fulfilling lives.

About the Illustrator

Úna Woods is an Illustrator from Dublin, Ireland. She loves to create magical illustrations for children using simple shapes, patterns and bright colours. Her first picture book 'Have You Seen The Dublin Vampire?' was published by The O'Brien Press in 2020. Her work has featured in children's books, educational books, print and web campaigns for clients such as Folens, Gill Education, Currach Books, HSE, The Irish Independent and many more. She is a member of Illustrator Guild of Ireland, Ibby and Children's Books Ireland. www.unawoods.com

Note to parents and teachers

This book introduces children to the mindfulness based practice of "Loving Kindness". The Loving Kindness practice encourages children to practise kindness towards themselves and others and to wish both themselves and others well. It also helps children build greater tolerance and empathy for others, especially those different from themselves.

When you are reading this book, ask your child to notice how they are both different and similar to other children they know. Explain that although we might look different on the outside, we all are similar on the inside. Explain that all people no matter what age, race or nationality feel sad, worried and angry sometimes and that all people want to feel happy, safe and loved.

Explain to your child that there is nobody in the world any better than they are, nobody any less and nobody the same. Tell them that just like the stars in the sky, each child is unique and special and to shine brightly like a star in the sky they need to do three things, be kind to themselves, be kind to others and to just try their best. Explain that they don't have to be the best, they just need to try their best and that is always good enough.

To guide your child in the "Kind Wishes" meditation, begin by inviting them to lie down and to close their eyes if they feel comfortable doing so. You can put some relaxing music on in the background and perhaps light a candle. Taking your time read through the guided "Kind Wishes" meditation script. When you are finished ask your child to notice how they feel inside after practising the meditation. Explain that this is how it feels when we wish kind things for ourselves and others.

You can also do this practice informally, perhaps making a wishing wand with a stick, paper stars and feathers. Ask your child to hold the wishing wand and first make a wish for someone they love, then make a wish for their family and friends, a wish for someone they don't know well, someone they find difficult to like and then perhaps for the whole world. You can also vary the wishes from time to time, for example, making a kind wish for all the children in their school, for animals or for the environment. Ask children to notice how it feels inside when they make kind wishes for themselves and others.

There are so many types of children
Different colours, shapes and size
We speak different types of languages
Have different hair and skin and eyes

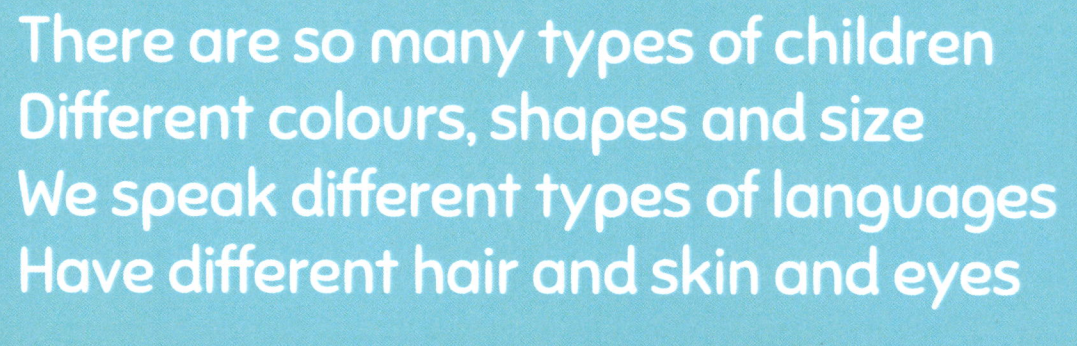

There are so many types of children
Too many different types to name
Outside we might look different
Though inside we're just the same

Sometimes, we all have struggles
We all want to have fun
We all want friends to play with
We all want to be loved

So when you play with other children
Remember to be kind
Outside they might look different
Though, we're all the same inside

So let's make a wish together
For all children near and far
Take a big deep breath
Put your hand onto your heart

May all of us live safely
May we live with joy and ease
May we be kind to one another
May our hearts be filled with peace

Notice how you feel now
Does your heart feel light?
When we wish nice things for others
It feels good for us inside

So when you meet with other children
Why not say this wish for them
It's sure to make you smile inside
It might just light up their day as well

Kind Wishes Meditation

When you are ready, you can lie down and close your eyes if you like.

Can you put your hand on your heart. Now, can you imagine your heart is glowing with a beautiful bright light? Imagine the light spreading all around you, so that you are surrounded by this warm, beautiful, shining light from your heart. Now, make some kind wishes for yourself, say to yourself, "may I be safe, may I be healthy, may I be happy, may I be really happy, may I be filled up with happiness from the top of my head to the tips of my toes".

Now, imagine this light from your heart spreading wider and growing stronger. Imagine all of your family in a circle around you. Let the light from your heart grow bigger and stronger so that all of your family is surrounded by this wonderful light. Now, make some kind wishes for your family, say to yourself, "may my family be safe, may they be healthy, may they be happy, may they be really happy".

Feel the light from your heart grow stronger, let it spread wider and wider. Imagine all of the children in your class, standing around you. Now, see your beautiful, bright light surrounding all of your friends and make some kind wishes for them, say to yourself, "may all of the children in my class be safe, may they be healthy, may they be happy, may they be filled up with happiness from the tops of their heads to the tips of their toes".

Now, imagine all of the people you know standing around you. See your light grow stronger and spread wider so that it surrounds all of these people. Make some kind wishes for them and say to yourself, "may all of the people I know be safe, may they be healthy, may they be happy, may they be really happy".

Feel the light from your heart grow even stronger, let it spread wider and wider. Now, imagine all of the people in your country standing around you. See your light spread so wide that it surrounds all of these people. Say to yourself, "may all of the people in my country be safe, may they be healthy, may they be happy, may they be really happy".

Now, feel the light from your heart grow even stronger, brighter and wider. Imagine all of the people in the world standing around you. See your light grow so strong and bright that it surrounds all of the people in the world. Say to yourself, "may all of the people in the world be safe, may they be healthy, may they be happy, may they be filled up with happiness from the tops of their heads to the tips of their toes".

Can you notice how you feel now? How does your head feel? How does your body feel? How does your heart feel? See can you notice the feeling around your heart for a few more moments. This is what it feels like when we make kind wishes for ourselves and others. Now, wiggle, wiggle your toes and slowly, slowly open your eyes.

Activity 1A

Outside we might look different but we're all the same inside

In the children draw, write or colour the different types of feelings that all children have.

Activity 1B

All families are different, all families are special, all families are important

In the houses draw four different types of families.

Activity 1C

Making Kind Wishes

Make a kind wish for your family

Make a kind wish for someone you don't know well

Make a Kind wish for Yourself

Make a kind wish for your friend

28

Activity 10

When we wish nice things for others we feel good inside

In the child draw, write or colour how you feel in your body when you make kind wishes for other children.

Testimonials

"Louise Shanagher is a leading voice in children's mental health, and her charming books offer young children a deep introduction to gratitude, compassion and mindfulness."

Dr Chris Willard,
Harvard Psychologist, Author,
World leading expert in Mindfulness for Children

"Once again Louise Shanagher has produced a beautifully written series of books with her new 'Kindfully Me' series. The simplicity of the rhymes, the lovely illustrations, and the powerful messages about kindness, compassion, acceptance and gratitude will be loved by children and parents alike. Perfect for the classroom or for bedtime, 'Kindfully Me' is a wonderful introduction to mindfulness meditation for young children."

Dr Mary Ó Kane, Parenting Expert and Psychology Lecturer

"The 'Kindfully Me' series makes me feel all warm inside as I sense calm and compassion radiating from each and every page. Louise has a unique way of nurturing important qualities in children, such as practising kindness towards others and towards ourselves, becoming aware of and accepting our colourful rainbow of emotions, and feeling thankful for what we have, all of which sow the seeds for emotionally healthy adults. The illustrations beautifully bring these qualities to life, and the practical activities are the perfect accompaniment to help children apply these qualities in their own lives. My little girls are delighted to have found a sequel to their treasured 'Mindfully Me' series which they feel from the top of their heads to the tips of their toes! Thank you Louise and Úna for this little piece of magic, which is sure to help children all over the world feel a sense of self-worth and belonging."

Dr. Malie Coyne,
Clinical Psychologist and Author of
'Love in, Love out: A compassionate approach to parenting your anxious child'